D1581075

Dinosaur RAP

Written by **John Foster**   Illustrated by **Debbie Harter**
Sung by **Mikey Henry Jr.**

Barefoot Books

60000484618

Come on everybody, shake a claw.
Let me hear you bellow. Let me hear you **ROAR!**
Let me see you jump and **thump** and **tap.**
Come and join in! Do the **dinosaur rap!**

There's a **Saltopus** strutting, swaying to the beat,
Hopping and bopping and tapping his feet.

Tap your feet!

There's a huge **Shonisaurus** jumping like a whale,
Flapping her flippers and lashing her tail.

Come on everybody, shake a claw.
Let me hear you bellow. Let me hear you **ROAR!**
Let me see you **jump** and **thump** and **tap.**
Come and join in! Do the **dinosaur rap!**

There's a twisting, twirling **Apatosaurus**
Encouraging everyone to join in the chorus.

There's a **Stegosaurus** prancing along,
Swishing his tail as he joins in the song.

Swish your tail!

Come on everybody, shake a claw.
Let me hear you bellow. Let me hear you **ROAR!**
Let me see you jump and **thump** and **tap.**
Come and join in! Do the **dinosaur rap!**

There's a **Triceratops** who stamps and stomps
As she rocks and rolls through the prehistoric swamps.

There's a **Pteranodon** swooping and diving,
Laughing at the dinosaurs jumping and jiving.

There's a **Tyrannosaurus Rex** giving mighty roars,
Stamping to the beat as he clicks his claws.

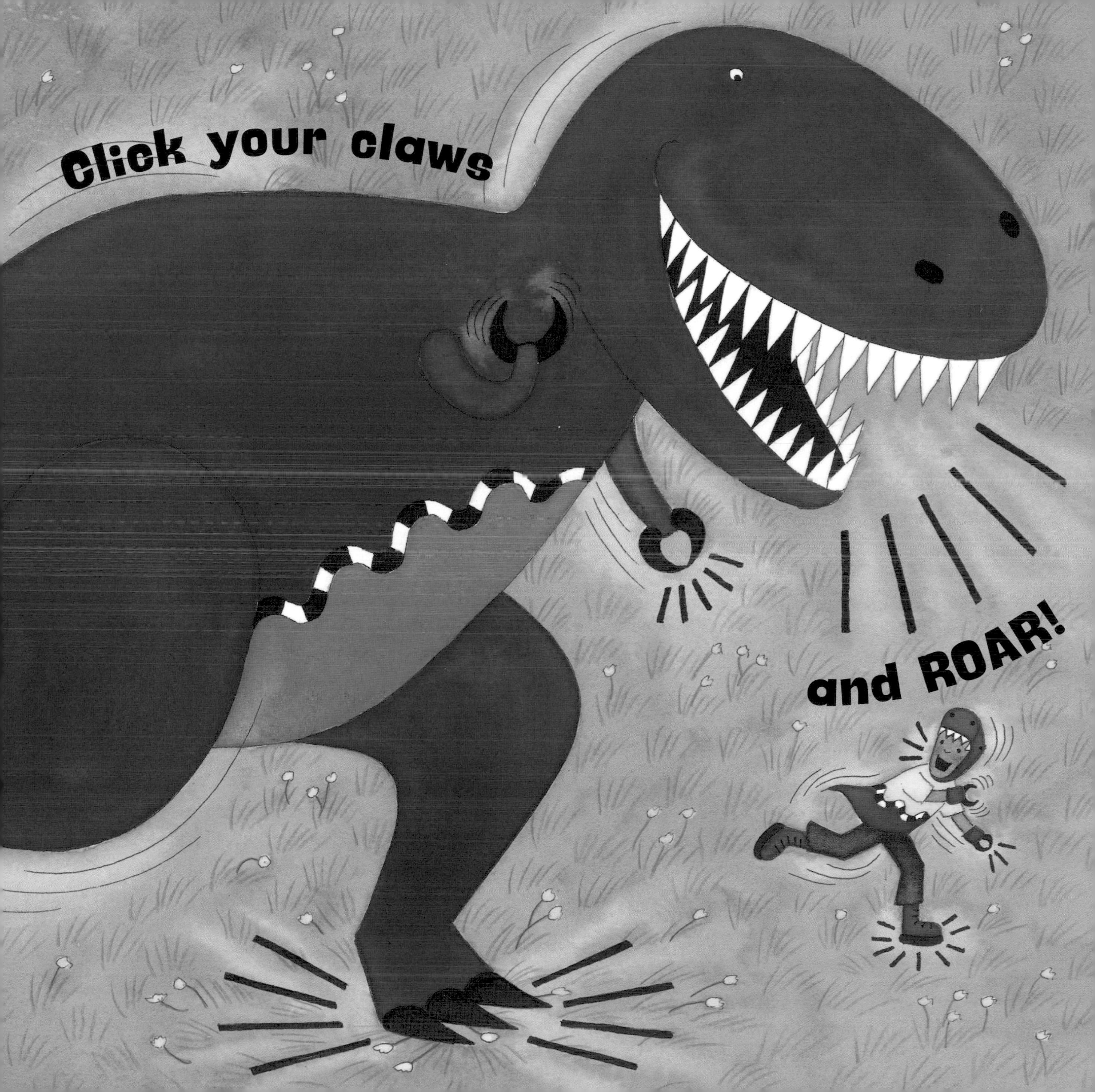

Click your claws

and ROAR!

Come on everybody, shake a claw.
Let me hear you bellow. Let me hear you ROAR!
Let me see you jump and thump and tap.
Come and join in! Do the dinosaur rap!

There are dinosaurs here. There are dinosaurs there.
There are dinosaurs dancing **everywhere!**
So swing your tails and shake your claws.
Rap around the planet with the **dinosaurs!**

Who's Who?

Saltopus (SALT-oh-pus)

Saltopus was one of the first dinosaurs. It walked on two legs and was about the size of a cat. It had a long head and dozens of small, sharp teeth that it used to tear and chew meat.

Shonisaurus
(show-ne-SORE-us)

Shonisaurus was the largest of the marine reptiles, a group known as the ichthyosaurs. It could grow up to 50m (160ft) long and be as big as a submarine. It looked like a cross between a dolphin and a whale. It was a slow swimmer and relied on its size and strength to catch its prey.

Apatosaurus
(a-pat-oh-SORE-us)

Apatosaurus had a long neck, but a small head. It was a herbivore and only had about 24 teeth. It may have swallowed stones to help grind up leaves in its stomach, because its teeth were too weak to chew all of the plants it ate.

Pteranodon (ter-AN-oh-don)

Pteranodon, although a very close relative of the dinosaurs, was actually a flying reptile and not technically a dinosaur. Many scientists believe that the Pteranodon, which was completely toothless, may have hunted like modern-day pelicans, scooping up fish off the water and swallowing them in one big gulp.

Stegosaurus (steg-oh-SORE-us)

Stegosaurus had a tiny brain the size of a walnut. It had spikes on its tail, which it used as a club to defend itself, because it could only run at about 7kph (4.5mph), about as fast as an Australian tiger beetle. It also had plates on its back to help it keep cool in the hot, humid weather.

Triceratops (tri-SER-ah-tops)

Triceratops was a bone-headed dinosaur with a large skull about 3m (10ft) long. It weighed between 6-12 tonnes (13,000-26,000 lbs) and had three horns on its head. It is believed to have lived in herds and would charge at its enemies like a rhinoceros.

Tyrannosaurus Rex
(tie-ran-o-SORE-us REX)

Tyrannosaurus Rex literally means "king of the tyrant lizards." It had an enormous skull with jaws as wide as a doorway and 50–60 fierce, razor-sharp teeth. Its breath must have stunk from the meat that got stuck in its teeth. It walked upright, but probably could not move very fast due to its huge size.

The Age of the Dinosaurs

The dinosaurs existed millions of years ago. The three periods during which they were alive are known as the Triassic era, the Jurassic era and the Cretaceous era.

During the Triassic era, Earth was covered in water all around, with a single landmass atop it known as Pangaea. The planet was hot and dry. This climate suited the reptiles that inhabited the land. Some reptiles, like the Shonisaurus, lived in the sea instead. At the end of this era, the first dinosaurs, such as the Saltopus, appeared. These were small, quick carnivores that walked on their hind legs.

During the Jurassic era, the climate became hot and humid, and the land was covered in forests. It then became two land masses, Gondwana and Laurasia, divided by a seaway called

Triassic Era (250 – 200 million years ago)

Jurassic Era (200

Some dinosaurs were as big as a double-decker bus, but others were small. The smallest was about the size of a crow. Some were fierce, meat-eating carnivores. Others, known as herbivores, ate only plants.

Tethys. Many mountain ranges were formed during this era. Large, four-legged dinosaurs appeared, such as the Apatosaurus and the Diplodocus. So did plated dinosaurs like the Stegosaurus.

During this period the land split into several continents and the climate was warm and muggy. Many of the flowers that we still find today first appeared during this era. Dinosaurs of all shapes and sizes roamed the earth's forests — fierce carnivores such as the Tyrannosaurus Rex, horned dinosaurs such as the Triceratops and plated dinosaurs such as the Ankylosaurus.

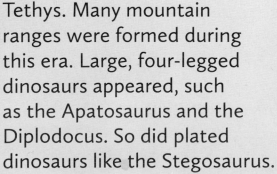

5 million years ago)   **Cretaceous Era (145 – 65 million years ago)**

What Happened to the Dinosaurs?

Even though the dinosaurs died millions of years ago, over time some of their buried bones were covered in layers of mud, so their skeletons didn't always fall apart. Instead, the bones became fossils. Fossils are bones or other body parts that have been preserved over long periods of time in stone, mud or other natural elements.

Fossils tell us a lot about dinosaurs. In fact, without fossils, we would not even know that dinosaurs had ever existed. We still do not know for certain why they died out and became extinct. Many scientists believe that they became extinct after a large meteorite hit the earth and a huge cloud of dust blotted out the sun. Others think that they died out because of climate change and the breaking apart of the earth's continents. Research scientists are still trying to find out the exact reason to this day.

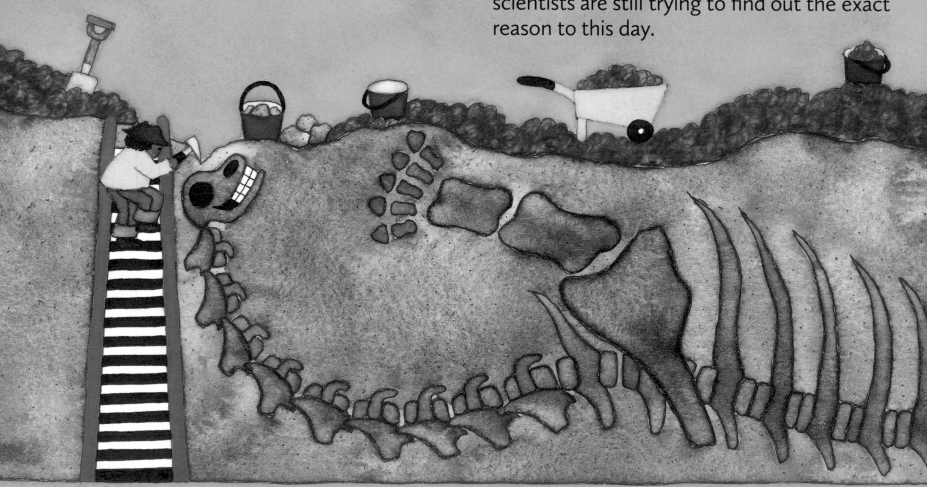

Tertiary Era (65 – 1.6 million years ago)

Digging Up Bones

Paleontologists are scientists who unearth and study fossils to learn more about the past. They use many tools to dig the fossils out of the earth: shovels, picks and even bulldozers to get through big chunks of rock and earth; trowels and digging knives to get closer to the bones; and delicate tools like paintbrushes to remove dirt from the fossils.

When all the bones have been dug up, the scientists measure and photograph each fossil and take notes about where it was found. They protect the bones by covering them in plaster jackets like the ones doctors use on broken bones in people. The fossils are then transported back to laboratories so the scientists can study them more carefully. Sometimes, copies are made of the bones to create replicas of dinosaurs for display in museums.

Quarternary Era (1.6 million years ago – present)

For Chris — J. F.
To Millie, Finley and Oliver — D. H.

Barefoot Books
23 Bradford Street, 2nd Floor
Concord, MA 01742

Barefoot Books
29/30 Fitzroy Square
London, W1T 6LQ

Text copyright © 2016 by John Foster. Illustrations copyright © 2016 by Debbie Harter
The moral rights of John Foster and Debbie Harter have been asserted

Musical composition and lead vocals © 2016 by Mikey Henry Jr.
Musical arrangement and mix © 2016 by Mikey Henry Jr. and Geoffrey Nielsen
Performed by Mikey Henry Jr. with additional instrumentation by Geoffrey Nielsen
Recorded at The Record Company, Boston, MA, USA. Mastered at M-Works Mastering Studio Inc, Cambridge, MA, USA
Animation by Sophie Marsh, Bristol, UK

First published in the United States of America by Barefoot Books, Inc and in Great Britain by Barefoot Books, Ltd in 2016
This paperback edition first published in 2021. All rights reserved

Graphic design by Judy Linard (London, UK) and Barefoot Books. Art directed by Tessa Strickland, Barefoot Books
Reproduction by B & P International, Hong Kong. Printed in China on 100% acid-free paper
This book was typeset in Negrita Pro, CCClobberinTime, Johann and Calluna Sans
The illustrations were prepared in water-based paints, pen and ink, and crayon

Paperback with enhanced CD ISBN 978-1-78285-302-2
Paperback ISBN 978-1-64686-449-2
E-book ISBN 978-1-78285-474-6

Library of Congress Cataloging-in-Publication Data is available under LCCN 2016039281

British Cataloguing-in-Publication Data: a catalogue record for this book is available from the British Library

1 3 5 7 9 8 6 4 2

Go to *www.barefootbooks.com/dinosaurrap* to access
your audio singalong and video animation online.